GREEN EXIT

EXIT PLANNING FOR LAWN AND LANDSCAPE BUSINESS OWNERS

RONALD L. EDMONDS
The Principium Group

Second Edition

Copyright © 2012 Ronald L Edmonds and The Principium Group. All rights reserved.

No part of this publication may be reproduced, stored in a retrieval system, or transmitted, in any form, or by any means, electronic, mechanical, photocopying, recording, or otherwise, without the prior consent of the copyright holder.

The information included herein is general in nature. Nothing included herein is intended to constitute legal or accounting advice. Readers are encouraged to consult with appropriate professional advisors in connection with any transactions they may be considering.

The characters and companies in this book are purely fictional. Any similarities between them and real individuals or companies are purely coincidental.

ISBN: 1480069310
ISBN-13: 978-1480069312

This book is dedicated to my family. Whenever I get lost or confused, you remind me what it's all about.

Acknowledgments

This book would not have been possible without the support of my colleagues Richard Helling and Chris Martin of The Principium Group who offered both encouragement and constructive criticism.

I am eternally grateful for the support and encouragement of my partner, editor and proofreader, Kathryn Edmonds. Her efforts have greatly improved the final product.

Potions of this book originally appeared in *Green Industry Merger & Acquisition News*.

GREEN EXIT

CONTENTS

	Acknowledgments	v
	Contents	vii
	Foreword	ix
1	An Overview of Exit Planning	1
2	An Exit Planning Parable	7
3	Understanding Your Objectives	13
4	Understanding the Value of Your Business	21
5	Improving the Value of Your Business	33
6	Preserving the Value of Your Business	41
7	Knowing When the Time is Right	49
8	Exit Planning with More Than One Owner	57
9	Transferring Your Business to an Insider	63
10	Lawn Care Businesses	71
11	Design-Build Businesses	79
12	Landscape Maintenance Businesses	87
13	Other Green Industry Businesses	95
14	Franchised Businesses	103
15	The ESOP Option	109
16	Private Equity	115
17	Putting the Plan into Place	121
18	Choosing Advisors	127
19	An Exit Planning Checklist	137
	About the Author	143

Green Exit

FOREWORD

Green Exit is the culmination of our experience in dealing with hundreds of business owners within what we call the Green Industry – lawn, landscape and tree service companies, along with related businesses such as garden centers, nurseries and tree farms.

Usually, we hear from green industry business owners when they have made a decision to sell their businesses. Oftentimes, circumstances have made the decision for them. We know, however, that business owners will usually come far closer to achieving their objectives if they go through the exit planning process well before the time comes to actually sell their businesses. That is what this book is all about.

Successfully exiting a green industry business requires three things to come into alignment:

- The owner must be financially and mentally prepared to sell the business.
- The business must be ready to be sold.
- Market conditions must be conducive to completing a sale.

The first two of these requirements are within the power of the business owner to plan for and to affect. The third is entirely beyond the business owner's control and is subject to many factors, including general economic conditions and business cycles. The business owner within an effective exit plan addresses his or her own readiness and the business's readiness and is thus prepared when market conditions are right for a business exit.

Our hope is that the readers of this book take action to prepare themselves and their businesses so that, when the time comes, they are prepared and able to achieve their own objectives.

1

AN OVERVIEW OF EXIT PLANNING

Every business owner's ownership interest will change hands at some point during the business owner's lifetime or immediately thereafter, either voluntarily or involuntary. That change may include the sale of the business to a third party, the transfer of the business to family members or employees or the liquidation of the business. Most green industry business owners would agree that having an exit strategy or a plan for how the ownership interest will be transferred is a good idea. Few, however, have gone through the process of developing an exit or succession plan.

There are four basic steps in developing an exit plan: determining the owner's objectives, assessing the current value and marketability of the business, developing an action plan for preserving and enhancing the value and marketability of the business, and developing a plan for the sale or transfer of the business in the future.

The Objectives of the Owner

Before proceeding with developing the exit plan, the owner must determine what his or her objectives really are, including determining when he or she wants to sell the business, to whom he or she wants to transfer the business and what net cash flows he or she will require after the business is sold. Determining one's true objectives requires some soul searching and may require assistance from financial professionals.

Assessing the Current Value and Marketability of the Business

In order to determine the best way to reach the objectives of the business owner, it is necessary to assess the value and marketability of the business. Ultimately, the marketplace will determine the value of the business, but an assessment of the business's value and marketability are necessary in order to determine if a business sale can reasonably be expected to produce a result that will allow the owner to achieve his or her objectives.

A formal business valuation may or may not be necessary, depending on the intentions of the owner. For example, a formal valuation may be necessary for tax purposes if the transfer will be made to a family member or if a sale is to be made to an entity such as an employee stock ownership plan (ESOP). A formal business valuation may also be necessary in the context of a divorce or the dissolution of a business partnership.

An assessment of the cash flows of the business is a key component of valuing the business and is also a key factor in structuring a transfer to family members or employees. In addition, an assessment must be made of current market conditions and the best time to go to market. While there are several methods of arriving at a business's value, assessing the cash flow of the business is directly or indirectly a part of each method.

Developing a Plan to Preserve and Enhance the Value and Marketability of the Business

After assessing the value and marketability of the business, a plan can be developed to enhance value and marketability. This plan is based on an assessment of the value drivers of the business. Value drivers are usually related either to the long-term growth prospects of the business or to factors that reduce a prospective buyer's risk that the business will not perform as expected.

Put more simply, the plan addresses steps that can be taken to improve the value and marketability of the business. The good news is that in most cases the same steps that improve the value and marketability of the business in the long-term will improve the operations and growth prospects of the business as well. These factors may include management and employees, operational issues, the nature and quality of the customer base, financial controls, facility issues and tax planning, among others.

Developing a Plan for the Sale or Transfer of the Business

Based on the objectives of the owner, the assessment of the value and marketability of the business and the plan for improving value and marketability of the business, a plan can be developed for the sale or transfer of the business. This plan will include the process to be followed and the proposed timing. This plan will be revisited based on inevitable changes in the owner's objectives, the state of the business and market conditions until the time comes to execute the plan for the sale or transfer of the business.

In this book we will be examining in more depth each of the four steps in exit planning.

2

AN EXIT PLANNING PARABLE

Albert was a fairly typical small business owner. He had worked hard to build a respectable business. He never dreamed that in only twenty years, the business would have grown from a part-time lawn mowing service to a $7 million commercial landscaping business with well over 100 employees. Albert's business was, in many ways, a family business. His wife Sherry had run his office for years, although she had been backing away the last few years by training other office personnel. She had a hold on things by only spending an average of two days a week in the business. Albert's son Joe had worked in the business since he was 15. If the truth were known, he had worked in it almost since he could walk. He had spent his summer school vacations riding with his father as he supervised his five crews. Joe always planned to take over the business from his father at some point. They were unusually close, and Joe's objective was to allow his father to work a lot less but still direct the business as long as he wanted to. He would try to learn everything his father knew. There was never any question where he would go to school – he went to A&M and studied agribusiness with an emphasis on landscape construction and maintenance. Albert was thrilled. Handing over a successful business to his son was one of his life's major goals, and everything was in place. When Joe finished school, he was ready to be the operations manager for the business. Albert called him the vice president of operations. He liked the sound of that. Pretty good for a 23 year old!

Albert's plan was in action. He knew exactly where he was going. Joe would be there to help him make it all happen, and when the time came, he would be ready to take over.

While Joe was away at school, he met Sarah there. They had lots in common and shared many interests. She was even a student in the agriculture college. They became inseparable. Two years after college, Joe married Sarah, and she began to work in Albert's business part-time. Everyone knew children would be coming along soon. Albert thought this was all great.

Sarah was from a small town about 150 miles away. Her parents had a small farm and dairy operation. They were able to visit her parents regularly, and that was a good thing because Sarah was very close to her parents.

One day when Joe and Sarah were about five years out of college, the call came from her mother. Her father Bill had had a serious heart attack. Joe and Sarah rushed home to her parents. The news from the doctors was pretty good. Her dad would probably have a fairly complete recovery, especially if he quit smoking and got his weight down. However, they believed it was best for him to scale back and retire at once. Sarah's father was upset, and her mother was scared. What was she going to do? Who would run the farm? Could she sell it? What would happen to her livelihood?

As they drove to their home the next day, Joe and Sarah talked. Sarah had forgotten how much she liked the town she had grown up in. Joe liked it, too. What a great place to raise a family! And Sarah really wanted to help her mother out. They began to talk about moving to Sarah's hometown and taking over the family business there. The more they talked and thought, the better the plan seemed to them. It was almost perfect, except that Joe was very worried about telling Albert about the new plan.

When Joe told Albert about their plans, Albert controlled his anguish. He cared about Sarah's parents, too. He knew that Sarah's hometown would be a great place to raise a family.

But inside, Albert was thinking that his world was being torn inside out. He was about to lose his vice president of operations. His dream of an easy transition to retirement had just evaporated. And then one more thing hit him: What if he were the next one to have a heart attack? Who would help him and Sherry cope with a sudden change like that?

After reflecting a bit - and a long talk with Sherry - he realized this news was not so bad. He wasn't really ready to retire. He had some time left to develop and implement his new "exit strategy." It was, however, time to take the exit planning process seriously—and to develop contingency plans just in case things didn't work out like he expected again.

Green Exit

3

UNDERSTANDING YOUR OBJECTIVES

In this chapter, we will focus on what we consider to be the first step in effective exit planning, which is understanding your objectives.

Understanding your own objectives may not be quite as simple as it may appear. I thought it might be interesting to share some of the objectives people have told me that they have in exit planning:

- What I really want to do is pass the business on to my children, but I don't know how to make that work.

- My employees helped build this business, and I think the best thing for everyone would be for the employees to be able to own the business.

- The most import thing to me is that I have a secure retirement. I have to have enough money to be secure in retirement.

- I have a new job lined up and I am ready to slow down a bit, but I need to make plans to sell my business to make that happen.

UNDERSTANDING YOUR OBJECTIVES

- My partners and I don't really have the same objectives. One of them wants to retire, but the rest of us want to stay with the business for many years.

- I always planned to pass the business on to my son, but he doesn't seem interested at all now.

- I had always intended to pass the business on to my child, but he hasn't really demonstrated any real business aptitude, so I don't think that's going to work.

- I think I am close to having taken the business as far as I can on my own. If the business is to survive and thrive, it will need more capital than I can contribute, or it will need talent and leadership that I cannot provide.

- I don't really want to sell my business and my best guess is I still won't want to five years down the road, but I would like to know that I can have options if things change.

As varied as those comments may seem, they are really just the simple versions of objectives that most business owners commonly have. Many business owners have some combination of many of those concerns. The situation is often complicated by the fact that business partners who work together perfectly well in operating the business may have very different needs and objectives when it comes to exit planning, with different time frames, family issues, lifestyle issues, etc. to contend with.

Typically, objectives can be categorized as *financial* or *nonfinancial*. Financial objectives include an objective to realize a certain value for the business, to have a transaction result in a sufficient amount of monetary assets (or income) to support the seller's needs in retirement and to provide value to one's heirs at the time of death. Nonfinancial objectives may include such goals as seeing the business survive and prosper under new leadership, rewarding loyal employees and passing the business on to one's family.

Once you have wrestled with the idea of what your objectives are, it is time to quantify them. For example, if retirement is your objective, what level of assets or monthly cash flow will be required to achieve your retirement objectives, considering not just the business, but your other investments, including retirement funds and social security, if applicable? A similar analysis is necessary if you are contemplating a career shift or acquiring (or starting) a different business.

Usually, it is necessary to involve your accountant and your financial advisor in this process to make sure you really understand your situation and what your options may be. A facilitator can often help you understand your own objectives better. He or she can also coordinate the input of your various advisors and help synthesize the various factors as you build your plan to achieve your objectives.

An important thing to remember is that objectives change over time. You really need to revisit your objectives regularly to make sure the plans you have in place still match your objectives.

Ultimately, there are three objectives common to nearly all business owners:

1. To be able to exit the business on your own timetable.

How long do you as the business owner want to remain active in the business?

2. To exit the business financially stable.

How much money will it take for you as the business owner to be financially stable after you exit the business? Do you want to completely "cash out" of the business when you leave, or are you willing to receive a portion of the purchase price over time?

3. To transfer the business to a particular person or group of people.

As a business owner, you may want to transfer the business to a child, a partner or a key employee. You may want to transfer the business to a third party and realize top dollar for the business. You may also want to partially exit the business by selling a portion of your interest, retaining the balance and remaining active in the business.

Answering these questions and articulating your objectives is the first and probably the most important

Understanding Your Objectives

step in the exit planning process. If you don't understand your objectives, it is impossible to craft a plan to meet them.

The reality is that comparatively few business owners achieve their objectives from an exit planning perspective. The reason is quite simple – not enough energy was devoted to articulating those objectives and devising a plan to achieve them. The owners are then left with having events beyond their immediate control dictate the process by which they ultimately exit the business. They are left with the consequences of the lack of planning which may include being saddled with the burden of business ownership longer than desired and ultimately realizing less from a sale than would otherwise have been possible.

When is the best time to begin the exit planning process? The best answer is when you start or otherwise acquire a business. The second best answer is *now*.

… GREEN EXIT

4

UNDERSTANDING THE VALUE OF YOUR BUSINESS

Understanding the value of your business is a key component of the exit planning process because it defines the business that you will be exiting at some point. It is the beginning step in determining how to preserve and enhance the value until the planned or unplanned need to transition the ownership of the business.

Few topics are as poorly understood as business valuation. Despite common misperceptions, it is a complex topic that cannot be boiled down to simplistic formulas or rules of thumbs.

Different kinds of buyers will view the value of a business differently. As a result, to understand the value of a business, it is important to understand the type of buyer that is likely to be interested.

There are two broad categories of buyers, strategic buyers and financial buyers.

Strategic buyers are buyers who have a specific reason to consider a particular acquisition. Generally, they are looking for revenue or cost synergies with their existing businesses. Synergies are financial benefits from the combination.

Revenue synergies are situations where revenues are expected to rise from an acquisition more than the amount of the revenues of the business being acquired. This can happen when the acquisition brings a new service line to the acquiring company's existing customers or the acquiring company brings a new service line to the customers of the acquired business. This can be created from the opportunity to cross-sell to customers, or it can be even more likely when one of the businesses provides a service that has been outsourced by the other party. One example in which that might happen is if a landscape maintenance company that has historically outsourced fertilization and weed control acquires another company that provides this service in-house and immediately discontinues outsourcing.

Cost synergies are situations in which the total costs for the combined company after an acquisition go down. Cost synergies arise when there is a duplication of costs, such as administrative overhead, advertising costs, facility costs, etc., that may be eliminated or reduced when the businesses combine. These are usually easier to quantify than revenue synergies.

Financial buyers, on the other hand, view a potential acquisition essentially as a standalone investment and are primarily seeking a return on their investment and cash flow. Typically, these are long-term investors seeking a solid, well-managed business. These buyers usually do not make immediate significant changes, except in turnaround situations. They may be interested in an acquisition as a platform for additional acquisitions that will create synergies.

From a value perspective, strategic buyers may place a value on synergies, while the financial buyer would not. Therefore, in most cases, a strategic buyer will be willing to place a higher value on an acquisition target than a financial buyer would.

There are a number of approaches to valuing a business. The most common ones are asset value, comparable transaction value, income capitalization, discounted cash flow and multiples.

The asset value approach is based on the value of the assets of the business less its liabilities. This approach usually does not highly value the intangible assets of the business and may not reflect the growth prospects of the business. It is used primarily with asset-intensive businesses and companies without existing profits.

The comparable transaction value approach is based on comparing the business in question to similar companies that have sold analyzing the differences between the comparable sale and the subject business. This is similar to the approach most often used in real estate appraisals. The problem with this approach is that there is not a great deal of data available relative to comparable sales of small businesses. This approach requires a great deal of judgment.

The income capitalization approach is essentially the annuity value of the current cash flow. The net cash flow of the business is divided by a capitalization rate. This approach assumes stable, consistent cash flow. It is difficult to apply in the case of declining or increasing cash flows, although a higher capitalization rate can be used to account for higher risk. This approach is commonly used for commercial real estate under long-term lease and other situations in which cash flows are stable on a long-term basis.

The discounted cash flow approach requires a projection of operating cash flows into the future, typically at least five years, and then discounts those cash flows along with the terminal value at the end of the five years back to the present using a discount rate. This approach is usually the best method on a theoretical basis, but requires a great deal of effort, skill and judgment. This is an approach that can also give value to identified synergies. The projection of cash flows into the future requires estimates and assumptions. In addition, the selection of an appropriate discount rate reflecting the underlying risk of the transaction and the buyer's investment requirements requires a great deal of judgment.

The multiples approach applies a multiple to the acquired business's revenues, earnings before interest taxes and depreciation (EBITDA), free cash flows (EBITDA less capital expenditures) or seller's discretionary earnings (EBITDA plus the seller's compensation and perks). This is a rather simplistic valuation approach that is usually meaningful in the context of the cash flow a buyer actually projects to generate from an acquisition.

One often hears green industry business owners speak of business valuation in terms of multiples of revenues or cash flow. While it is absolutely true that offers for the purchase of a business, especially a recurring revenue business like lawn care and some lawn maintenance businesses, may be made in the form of a price per dollar of revenue, that offer is actually the result of the buyer's analysis and evaluation of the cash flow it can expect to generate from the acquisition. In practice, the multiple on revenue will be higher if a business has a higher margin than is typical in the industry and will be lower if the business has a lower margin. The multiple on cash flow will vary with a much more narrow range than the multiple on revenues.

In evaluating the cash flow that a buyer expects to generate from an acquisition, there are many factors to consider, including:

- The size of the business
- Historical profitability
- Record of growth
- Extent and condition of vehicles and equipment
- Service pricing
- Customer retention patterns
- Type of customer (residential, commercial, governmental)
- Revenue mix (recurring vs. nonrecurring)
- Customer concentrations
- The strength of the management team and employees
- The importance of the owner/seller's involvement in the business to its ongoing success
- The age of the business

- The geographic territory served
- The competitive environment

These factors will affect how the buyer evaluates the business and the risk associated with the buyer's ability to achieve the expected cash flows from the business. The greater the perceived risk of the business not continuing to generate the expected cash flows, the higher the discount rate or risk factor that seller will use in evaluating the cash flows and the lower the multiple of cash flow it will be willing to pay.

Some illustrations of this concept are as follows:

- A landscape services company with an aging fleet may receive a lower multiple than one with a newer fleet because the buyer will factor into its assessment of cash flows the need to update the fleet.

- A landscape company with a greater percentage of construction revenues will usually command a lower multiple because its revenues will be largely nonrecurring.

- A lawncare company with pricing lower than the market and lower than that charged by the buyer will usually receive a lower multiple.

- A lawncare company with a small number of relatively high dollar commercial accounts will usually command a lower multiple than a similarly sized company with a large number of small dollar residential customers because of the risks associated with the concentration. Losing one or two large customers may undermine the value of the potential acquisition.

- A company that has higher margins because it pays below-market compensation and benefits will command a lower multiple than one that pays similarly to the potential buyer.

Some buyers will evaluate the business based solely on how it performs on a stand-alone basis, while others will evaluate it based on how it expects to integrate the acquired operations into its own.

These factors partially account for the wide range of business valuations. In the lawn and landscape industry, the majority of transactions have been somewhere in the range of two to five times cash flow. That is a pretty wide range, and some transactions fall outside that range, particularly on the low end. It takes a very strong business to command a multiple at the high end of that range.

Ultimately, the market will value a business for sale. After all, fair market value is defined as "the price at which a property would change hands between a willing buyer and a willing seller when the former is not under any compulsion to buy and the latter is not under any compulsion to sell, and both parties have reasonable knowledge of relevant facts."

It is often desirable in the exit planning process, however, to obtain a business valuation or market assessment. The purpose of such a valuation is to estimate how the market will value the business when the time comes to sell. (There are other reasons to obtain a business valuation, and the purpose of the valuation is important to communicate to the valuator.) Competent business valuations can be prepared by a variety of professionals, including business appraisers and some CPAs and business brokers.

The business valuation process should also help a business owner to understand the value drivers of his or her business. Value drivers are those characteristics of his or her particular business that tend to increase the value (or multiple) assigned to the business. Negative value drivers are those characteristics that tend to decrease the value or multiple. Understanding those value drivers will enable the business owner to develop a plan to preserve and increase the value of the business over time. This will be the topic of a later chapter.

5

IMPROVING THE VALUE OF YOUR BUSINESS

Assuming you are not in a situation of having to take your business to market immediately, there are concrete steps that you as a business owner can take to improve the value and marketability of your business when you do plan to sell it.

Focusing on Earnings and Cash Flows

As discussed in the previous chapter, the most important (but not the only) factor in determining the value of your business is the cash flow that it generates. Steps taken to build the predictable sustained cash flow of the business over time will result in higher valuation and marketability.

Focusing on the Fundamentals

In building the cash flow from the business, it is a good idea to focus on the fundamentals of the business. A good place to start is to make a list of the strengths and weaknesses of the business, trying to see them through the eyes of a potential buyer. You can then develop an action plan to take advantage of the strengths and to minimize the impact of the weaknesses. Among the topics that may appear on that list are such items as:

Service lines

- Do the Company's service lines make sense and will they appeal to buyers?

- Are there services which should be added and others which should be eliminated?

Pricing strategies

- Does your pricing strategy support your overall business strategy?

- Do you have a pricing strategy?

Target markets and customers

- What are your target markets and who are your target customers?

- Do they make sense in the short-term and the long-term?

Physical locations

- Are the business's physical locations desirable?
- Should the business relocate or add additional locations?
- What can be done to make the business's existing locations more desirable?

Employees

- What can you do to improve employee quality and retention?
- Have you taken steps to protect the business from former employees (and future former employee)s soliciting clients and competing against the business?

When prospective buyers take a look at your business, they will want to know who the key employees are, how long they have been with the business and how likely it will be that these key employees will stay with the business after a sale is completed. They will also be interested in knowing how the business will be protected if some of these employees decide to leave and compete with the business.

Making Your Business Less Dependent on You

One key step is to consider how to make the success of the business less dependent on you as the owner. This can often be accomplished by a combination of implementing good systems and having high quality key employees you can empower to act in your absence. Accomplishing this will make it easier for prospective buyers to understand how the business can successfully transition from your ownership to theirs. It may also allow you to take a vacation.

Implementing Quality Administrative Systems and Procedures

One step in making the business run more smoothly and efficiently is to implement quality administrative systems and procedures. This may include such steps as developing a usable policy and procedures manual or implementing up-to-date computer systems.

Maintaining Good Financial Records

Maintaining good financial records is a significant key to the marketability of the business. Good records are both accurate and timely. They document the performance of the business over time. It is extremely difficult to sell a business, especially at a premium price, if high quality financial records are not available or are not prepared on a timely basis.

Maintaining a Distinction Between Your Business and Personal Affairs

One step in preparing a business for sale is to identify financial items (both income and expense, but usually mostly expenses) that will not apply to the new owners of the business. This may involve items of expense that are discretionary to the owners of the business and would not be required of a new owner. These items, commonly called add-backs, are a part of nearly all business sale transactions. However, the larger these items become as part of the business, the greater the scrutiny they will receive, and the harder it becomes to unlock the full value of the business.

Retaining Quality Advisors

Retaining quality legal, financial and other advisors as you build your business will help ensure that you structure your business in such a way that, when the time comes, it is possible to structure as favorable a transaction as possible. Your advisors will also already be available, and you will not be scrambling for advice and counsel late in the game.

These are just a few of the steps that you can take to improve the value and marketability of your business over time. The exit planning process should include an evaluation of your specific situation and a concrete set of steps you can take to improve the value and marketability.

Green Exit

6

PRESERVING THE VALUE OF YOUR BUSINESS

In many cases, exit planning begins long before an exit event actually happens, either planned or unplanned. In fact, traditional wisdom suggests that exit planning should begin the day you start or buy a business. Therefore, there may be a significant time lag from the point that you first begin exit planning and the time that plan is executed. In earlier chapters, we have focused on understanding the value of your business and improving the value of your business over time. In this chapter, we focus on preserving the value of your business prior to completing an exit strategy.

A good way to begin assessing how to preserve the value of the business is to ask what risks the company faces that might affect its value between the present time and a planned exit point. Of course the business world is full of risks – some we can control, and some we can't.

What if something happens to you as the business owner that prevents you from devoting your time to the business either temporarily or permanently? Some examples would include your death or disability or your need to focus on other issues, such as the health of a family member.

Is your business so dependent on the continued services of one or more key employees that the business would be severely impacted as a result of their absence? The same things that could happen to you as a business owner could happen to a key employee. In addition, they might simply decide to leave for a whole host of reasons, one of which could actually be to compete with you.

Many risks that threaten the value of the business are related to the business owner having mentally made a decision to exit the business and, therefore, becoming complacent about competitive threats and marketplace shifts or hesitant to make the investments required to achieve the potential of the business.

Of course, there are the traditional risks, many of which may be insurable or controllable, to consider. This is not a time to skimp on insurance and risk management.

Many of us focus on what would happen in the event of our death. However, for a typical 40 to 50-year old business owner, the risk of becoming disabled is approximately twice the risk of dying during your remaining time in the active workforce. We usually think about the adequacy of life insurance and disability insurance to meet your family's needs in the event of your death or disability, but meeting the needs of your business in the event of your death or incapacity may be a key step in preserving its value as your most important asset.

Business continuity planning has the goal of making sure your business can continue to operate, not only after a natural calamity but also in the event of other disruptions, including illness or departure of key employees, supply chain issues or other challenges that businesses face from time to time. It can prove a valuable part of preserving the value of your business.

Here are some important questions to ask yourself as a business owner:

- Do you have a written plan for your business if something unexpected happens to you? Have you thought about what would be best for your business and your family in this event?

- Have you identified a person who can manage the business in your absence? This person could be a family member, a key employee or perhaps even a competitor. The key here is to identify this person, gain his or her agreement and make it known in some fashion that this is your desire.

- Have you identified a person who can oversee the finances of your business in your absence? This person could be a family member, a key employee or perhaps your accountant or another professional advisor?

- What would be the impact of your death, disability or absence on your business's financing arrangements?

- Do you have a specific written strategy or plan to retain employees critical to the operation of the business if you can no longer be active in the business due to death, disability or other reasons.

- If you have partners, do you have a current buy-sell agreement in place? Is it backed by a method of financing the buy-sell transaction, e.g. insurance?

- Have you communicated your continuity plan to key employees?

A business continuity plan is on many business owners' to-do lists. Well, maybe it is on at least a few business owners' to-do lists. With the pressure of day-to-day operations and the rest of life's obligations, it rarely makes it to the top of the list. In the context of exit strategy planning, the need to preserve the value of your business in order to achieve your exit strategy objectives becomes extremely significant and should not be ignored. There is no quicker way to destroy the value of a business than to remove its visionary leader, its manager, and often its chief sales person without a well thought-out plan for dealing with the void that is left behind.

Preserving the Value of Your Business

We often tell clients that the single most important thing they can do to improve their prospects for the sale of their business is to make sure it is continuing to operate on all cylinders and to avoid getting so wrapped up in the process of the sale of the business that they lose their edge with the business itself. A business that is stagnant, is not growing or does not react to changes in the market will not be nearly as attractive an acquisition target.

Timing your exit is a complex process. For the most optimum result, your business has to be ready; you, as a business owner, have to be ready; and market conditions have to be right. Because those things don't always happen at the same time, additional risks enter into the equation. While those risks certainly cannot be completely controlled, taking steps like those we've recommended here can help make it more likely that when you are ready to sell your business and market conditions are right, your business will be ready as well.

Green Exit

7

KNOWING WHEN THE TIME IS RIGHT

Almost everyone knows that there will come a time to transition the ownership of their business, whether by a sale to a third party or a transition of ownership to employees or family members. For some business owners, this will come on an involuntary basis due to death, disability or other pressing matters. However, most business owners have the opportunity to plan for that transition with the goal of making the transition happen "when the time is right."

Some business owners have a clear idea of when the time will be right for them. Perhaps it is when some business milestone is reached, such as attaining a certain level of sales. For some, it may be when they have built the infrastructure of the business to a certain level. For others, it may be when they determine that their designated successor, perhaps a trusted employee or family member is ready.

There are really two dimensions to being ready to sell your business. You really need to be both financially ready and mentally ready. Let's explore these two dimensions.

What does it mean to be financially ready to sell or transfer your business? Basically, it means you have evaluated the likely outcome of the sale or transfer process in the context of your particular financial situation.

In the case of a sale or transfer in the context of retirement, the operative question is will the after-tax proceeds of the sale of the business (or the cash flow streams associated with its transfer), together with your other assets and income streams (retirement accounts, social security, etc.), meet your lifestyle and other requirements in retirement?

If the context is not retirement, the question remains – will the sale or transfer of the business allow you to meet your objectives?

In order to answer these questions, you will need the help of professional advisors to assist in understanding the value of your business as well as the tax consequences of various options.

Determining whether or not you are mentally ready to sell your business can be an even more complicated question. When we first have a conversation with potential business sellers, we usually ask them if they are ready to sell their business. The answer is inevitably yes. After all, why else would they be talking to us about it? The reality is that many business owners do not realize how mentally unready they are to sell their business.

Here are some questions to ask yourself in assessing your mental readiness to sell your business:

- Do you still enjoy providing the day-to-day leadership of the business?

- Is the business dependent on you for day-to-day leadership?

- Can you envision yourself saying, "If you want something done right, you have to do it yourself"?

- Is it difficult for you to accept the idea of the business that you have built under someone else's leadership?

- Is it hard for you to envision what you will be doing after the sale of the business?

- Are you dependent on the perks of business ownership for maintaining your lifestyle?

If you answered these questions yes, you may not be mentally ready to sell your business. On the other hand, yes answers to the following questions may indicate that you are mentally ready to sell your business:

- Do you enjoy working but look forward to the time when working is optional?

- Do you have a new career opportunity that you are anxious to get involved with following the sale of your business?

- Do you feel pressure or a desire to spend more time with your family?

- Do you have outside interests that will occupy your time if you are considering retirement in connection with the sale of your business?

So what can you do if there is a question of whether you are ready, either financially or mentally, to sell your business?

If you are not financially ready for the sale of your business, some of the things you may want to consider include:

- Delaying your planned exit until you can financially prepare.

- Reconsidering lifestyle decisions following the sale of the business, making sure they are realistic for the circumstances.

- Taking steps to grow your business and improve its value and marketability between now and the time you would really like to exit the business.

If you are not mentally ready for the sale of the business, some of the steps you may want to consider include the following:

- Developing your management team with the objective of your being less critical to the day-to-day operations of the business.

- Creating a separation between your business and personal affairs.

- Developing outside interests.

- Pursuing post-sale career opportunities.

Realistically assessing your readiness for selling your business is an important step early in the exit planning process. This will help you to avoid pursuing opportunities that aren't really realistic given your current situation, while allowing you to make business and personal changes that will facilitate the process and help achieve the best possible results in the future.

Green Exit

8

EXIT PLANNING WITH MORE THAN ONE OWNER

Every day, it happens to somebody in the green industry. Events dictate that they must leave a business that they have owned, either individually or as a part of some form of partnership. The reasons range from critical ones, such as illness, disability, divorce or other family matters, to a desire for a change of vocation or location. Oftentimes, it may be triggered by the simple fact that partners, for whatever reasons, don't want to be partners anymore.

Whether or not one is the sole owner of his business or one of several partners, it is a given that one day he will want to (or need to) exit the business. That situation is usually complicated and often stressful under the best of scenarios. When the business has more than one owner, the issues multiply.

While business partnerships are very common, partners may have very different personal situations and perspectives, which may make planning for the exit of one partner very difficult.

Several questions come to mind:

Exit Planning With More Than One Owner

- If one partner wants to or needs to leave the business, will the remaining owners (or the business itself) be obligated to buy him or her out?

- If a partner does leave the business, can he or she compete against the existing business?

- How will the business be valued for the purposes of buying out a partner?

- How will the buy-out be financed? Will the partner be paid out in cash or in installments over time?

- How will the inevitable disagreements be resolved?

- What if one partner believes the time is right to sell the business and another doesn't?

These questions are best addressed when the business is formed or acquired (or when a new owner is added). An agreement among the partners covering these topics is called a "buy-sell agreement."

Even when a buy-sell agreement is already in place, it is a good idea to review where a business stands with its owners regularly and to update the agreement based on changing circumstances. The complexity of the buy-sell agreement is likely to increase as the business is successful and grows.

It is particularly important to address how the obligations under a buy-sell agreement will be funded under various circumstances. For example, it is rather uncommon for a small business in this industry to be able to self-fund a cash buyout of a partner. In the current lending environment, it may also be very difficult to borrow the funds to buy out a partner. It may be necessary to make the buyout a payment over time funded from the business's cash flows. In some cases, insurance can play a role. It is fairly common for a business to use life insurance to fund the business's obligations under a buy-sell agreement in the event of the death of a partner. But, of course, death is only one of many situations that a buy-sell agreement must address. For example, in many cases the risk of one partner becoming disabled is far greater than of a partner dying.

The objectives of the buy-sell agreement include producing a fair result to all of the owners of the business and preserving the value of the business for its owners, both those who will remain with the business and those who will exit. Achieving those objectives requires planning on the front end. It also requires regular updates to make sure that the plan that made sense when the agreement was written still makes sense in the present and can be executed when the time comes.

GREEN EXIT

9

Transferring Your Business to an Insider: Another Parable

Jay was struggling as he pondered the future. His lawn and landscape business had grown to be one of the dominant landscape companies in the city. He was extremely proud of what he had accomplished in a little over 25 years. He knew that it was time for him to develop his exit plan, but he wasn't sure what direction to steer the business, JPO Landscape.

Jay had always dreamed of passing JPO Landscape on to his son Adam, but he had some real concerns about that idea. It wasn't that he didn't think Adam had aptitude for the business. As a matter of fact, he was pretty sure Adam had even more aptitude for the business than he had had at Adam's age. His big concern was that nearly all of his wealth was tied up in JPO. He was counting on it to finance his retirement. In addition, he had become quite comfortable with the perks that come along with ownership of a successful business. Jay had been approached a few times with offers to buy his business. None of those opportunities particularly excited him, but he knew that a third party sale would probably come the closest to meeting his financial requirements as he considered retirement.

Many green industry business owners face a similar conundrum. After building a successful business, they would like nothing more than to be able to pass that business on to either a family member or, perhaps, to one or two key employees who have contributed to the growth of the business. On the other hand, many business owners have the vast majority of their resources tied up in the business. They are dependent on the cash flow from the business to sustain their lifestyle.

Because the business is so crucial to the owner's financial plans, transferring the business to an insider may seem like an impossible situation. Consider the following:

- Few insiders would have the liquid resources to buy the business out right at a competitive price.

- A transaction with insiders will usually not produce the synergies that can help command the highest price.

- You can't really judge the insider's management skills and commitment to the business.

- You may lose control of the business before you have been completely cashed out and feel comfortable that the business can thrive under the new ownership.

On the other hand, there may be compelling reasons to consider a transfer of the business to a family member or key employee:

- It is a way to keep the business in the family. Many business owners yearn to see their heirs maintain the success of the business.

- It can be a way to motivate and reward key employees.

- The business owner may be able to gradually scale back his or her day-to-day involvement in the business during the transition process, while maintaining a level of involvement and control.

- A transaction with an insider will often prove far less traumatic for employees and customers alike.

- There is a possibility to structure a transaction that can be tax-advantaged and yield substantial cash flow to the seller over time.

- Insiders may be more open-minded than third parties to possible alternative structures, such as a stock sale versus an asset sale.

There are a variety of options to consider in structuring an insider sale. It can involve a sale of stock, a sale of assets, a step transaction over time and, in some cases, may involve an employee stock ownership plan (ESOP).

Planning the sale of a business to a family member or key employee can be a complicated process and one that will take time to successfully execute. The plan needs to have the following characteristics:

- It needs to meet the existing owner's financial requirements.

- It needs to be fair to both the existing and new owners.

- It needs to be structured to minimize the tax burden.

- It needs to position the business for continued success under its new owners.

Balancing all of those characteristics is a tall order, but not impossible with a little time, flexibility and the assistance of quality legal, tax, accounting and transaction advisors. With time, planning and the right advisors, business owners like Jay often have the opportunity to meet their financial objectives while also achieving their non-financial goals for the transition of the business.

The good news for Jay is that he still has options and time to plan for both retirement and the ultimate transfer of his business, whether it is to his son, another insider or to a third-party in a sale on the open market. In order for him to achieve his objectives, however, he does need to begin the planning process and take concrete steps to enhance the value and marketability of his business.

Green Exit

10

Lawn Care Businesses

In this chapter, we will explore issues unique to lawn care companies. In this context, lawn care companies refers to businesses whose principal focus is providing lawn fertilization and weed control services. The lawn care industry has grown dramatically over the past 30 years. The industry comprises a very wide range of businesses, from mammoth industry leader TruGreen, with one billion dollars in annual revenue, to much smaller local businesses, some with annual revenues of less than one hundred thousand.

Lawn care companies come in a wide range of flavors. Many focus primarily on residential customers, while others primarily serve large commercial accounts, including office buildings, homeowners' associations and athletic fields.

As concerns about the use of fertilizers and pest control products have grown, many companies have responded by adopting more environmentally friendly practices. Some have adopted the use of organic products. Others, while still using chemicals have moved toward organically-based products. Still others have adopted integrated pest management approaches which attempt to minimize the use of chemicals.

Lawn care companies typically sell their customers a package program which includes a fixed number of treatments (or applications) of fertilization and weed control per year, along with a variety of add-on services, which might include such things as core aeration, grub and insect control and, in some markets, fire ant control. Services are either provided on an annual contract basis, which may be formal or informal, or, quite typically, on a continuing service-until-cancelled basis. Sometimes add-on services are sold as part of the program and provided like basic services on a continuing-until-cancelled basis. In other situations, they are sold each year.

Over time, several large companies have developed which have served to consolidate the market. Notable among these companies are TruGreen, a unit of The ServiceMaster Company, and Scott's Lawn Care, a part of the Scott's Miracle-Gro Company. TruGreen's pathway to becoming the industry leader has included numerous acquisitions, including ChemLawn and

Barefoot Grass, along with a host of local lawncare companies in many parts of the United States and Canada. Scott's has also completed many local lawncare company acquisitions, although it has not been active with acquisitions recently.

The lawncare industry also includes a wide range of franchised businesses. Both TruGreen and Scott's are active as franchisors. There are a great many other lawn care franchisors, including Lawn Doctor, Naturalawn, Spring Green and Weed Man, among many others.

The existence of the consolidators in the market has tended to increase the valuations of lawn care companies. As strategic buyers, these consolidators have tended to bid up the value of lawn care targets, especially during periods in which more than one consolidator has been active. This phenomenon has also contributed to a significant variability in valuations. Valuations have tended to fall during periods in which there have been fewer consolidators active in the market, a situation which has proven disappointing to many potential sellers. During periods of economic uncertainty, the consolidators have tended to be more disciplined in their valuations.

Franchise owners have tended to realize lower values for their businesses than have independent business owners. This is true even though franchise businesses are sometimes more profitable than independent businesses. The values of the franchises have been held down by the restrictions associated with franchise agreements, including territorial limitations, covenants not to compete, requirements for franchisor approval of transferees and, in many cases, a right of first refusal by the franchisor which may tend to limit the interest of third-party potential buyers.

The following value drivers are particularly significant for lawn care companies:

- The amount of annual recurring revenue.
- The proportion of annual recurring revenue that is from basic services versus add-on services.
- The growth rate of annual recurring revenue.

- The company's pricing structure, including history of price increases.//
- The stability and age of the customer base.
- The retention rate of customers.
- The mix of customers between residential and commercial.
- The density of the customers (allowing more efficient employee scheduling).
- The quality of employees and management.
- The Company's selling methods.
- Company image and reputation.
- Compliance issues.

Like all companies, it is highly desirable for lawn care company owners considering selling their business in the future to go through the process of readying their business for sale well in advance of their desired exit time frame. This process will enable them to take advantage of market fluctuations and sell at or near the top of the business cycle. Because of the role of consolidators in this market and their tendency to value acquisitions on a strategic basis, variations in valuation over the course of the business cycle have tended to be significant.

11

Design-Build Businesses

In many ways, design-build companies are right at the heart of what the landscape industry is all about – creating beautiful outdoor environments for businesses, residences and public spaces. They are at the forefront of significant trends such as sustainable landscaping, green roofs and outdoor living spaces. This segment of the industry has attracted many of the most talented people in the industry, and their work is often an enduring legacy to their creativity, resourcefulness and commitment to the environment.

That being said, design-build companies present some challenges when it comes to exit planning. Other segments of the lawn and landscape industry tend to have recurring revenue, which is typically highly prized by consolidators and other buyers. Design-build companies, by their very nature, tend to have little, if any, recurring revenue. As a result, valuations tend to be lower than in other industry segments.

Because of these issues, design-build companies are often encouraged to build a recurring revenue maintenance business. We agree that adding recurring maintenance revenues makes sense for many design-build companies. Maintaining the projects they create helps ensure the long-lasting value of the projects. In addition, the recurring revenue associated with maintenance will help build and preserve value of the business. We do not agree that design-build companies necessarily do not have much value.

Design-build companies are similar in many ways to other non-recurring revenue service businesses. While they will rarely command the valuation multiples associated with recurring revenue businesses, these companies can be very salable. Focusing on the specific value drivers associated with design-build companies will help them become more salable and move valuations up the range of possible values.

Like other segments of the industry, design-build companies include a wide range of types of businesses. Many serve a primarily residential market, many have commercial clients and many serve both segments.

Some of the key drivers of business value for design-build companies include the following:

- A business reputation apart from the business owner.

- A demonstrable system for generating new business, again independent of the owner of the business.

- The quality, profitability and stability of the customer base.

- The track record of repeat business and referrals from existing customers.

- High quality employees involved in sales and in the field.

- The quality of the management and employees.

- The buyer's probability of being able to retain management and employees.

- The attractiveness of the business's physical facilities and equipment.

- The diversity of the Company's products and services. The design-build business may consider adding such services as irrigation, hardscapes, swimming pools, etc. that complement its core business.

- The development of special niche service lines which have minimal competition.

- The quality of the business's financial information.

- Where possible, structuring services in as standard a way as possible.

- Well-designed and documented systems for all phases of the business.

- Where it makes sense, adding recurring revenue services that complement the underlying business, including maintaining landscape projects that the company designs and builds.

The key to improving the salability and value of a design-build business is to focus on those value drivers that the business owner can affect.

Because the demand for design-build businesses tends to be lower than for recurring revenue businesses, it may be very helpful to consider some additional techniques which may enable the owner to realize a higher value.

Being flexible with the structure of a possible transaction will tend to increase the value of the business. For example, seller financing generally increases the value of the business in the eyes of a potential buyer. The more of the purchase price the seller is willing to finance, the higher the price will likely be. Although seller financing is rarely, if ever, the first choice of a business seller, the results can be dramatic. Needless to say, the structure of any seller financing is extremely important to protect the interests of the seller. That being said, positioning the design-build business in such a way that seller financing of some degree is an option can be a very positive move.

In terms of transaction structure, it is very important to consider the net after tax impact of the transaction. In some situations, a lower sales price may be offset by positive tax impacts of a transaction structure. For example, if a business is structured as a C corporation, a seller might be well advised to offer a lower sales price if a buyer is willing to consider buying the stock of the corporation, which could result in a much lower total tax burden on the seller.

Another option that should be seriously considered by design-build business owners is a sale to the company's employees, either directly or through an employee stock ownership plan (ESOP). While such transactions tend to be at lower valuations than third-party transactions, they can offer substantial tax benefits and allow the seller to maintain a level of control through the process that may not be available in a third-party transaction. In addition, the employees involved may more clearly see the value of the business, despite the fact that it has little recurring revenue. The risks to the buyer are lower because they are already involved in and understand the business.

Because the market is limited for design-build businesses, early and careful planning are appropriate. Some possible transactions, such as an ESOP, may require a substantial amount of time to execute.

Green Exit

12

LANDSCAPE MAINTENANCE BUSINESSES

Landscape maintenance companies cover a wide range of business operations, some operating in the business-to-business segment and others operating in the business-to-consumer segment. These segments have substantially different characteristics, but all of these businesses focus primarily on recurring revenue business models.

There are many large companies operating in the commercial segment, ranging from such industry giants as The Brickman Group, the ValleyCrest Companies and TruGreen Landcare to large regional players to relatively small, locally-owned businesses. While smaller local companies perform a great deal of commercial work, many commercial accounts require the resources that a larger company offers, such as the ability to cover a wide geographical territory and the ability to guarantee performance on a level that is hard for a small company to achieve. While the barriers to entry associated with commercial services are higher than for residential services, they are certainly not enormous, and new entrants are able to enter the market frequently, increasing competition. Commercial accounts tend to always be looking for higher standards of performance at the most competitive pricing. Commercial landscape services companies may focus on one or more types of customer – office buildings, warehouses, educational institutions, homeowners associations, governmental entities, etc.

Residential landscape maintenance also covers a wide range of types of businesses. These businesses include firms aimed at high-end "estate" customers, upper middle class neighborhoods and lower-end businesses. Firms targeting upper middle class neighborhoods tend to provide a wide range of landscape maintenance services, including leaf removal, mulching, seasonal color and the like. The lower-end market includes so-called "mow, blow and go" companies that often advertise a low price, achieving profitability by efficient operations and customer density. Particularly at the lower end of the residential market, there is a good bit of competition from part-time workers who provide mowing services as a second job and, to some degree, teenagers.

Landscape maintenance companies also vary widely in their scope of services. Some provide full-scale landscape construction services. Many others do not. At a minimum, most commercial landscape maintenance companies provide enhancement services, partially as an accommodation to their customers. Landscape maintenance companies may also provide some of the following services:

- Irrigation system installation and service
- Fertilization and weed control
- Snow removal services
- Other exterior maintenance services

Landscape maintenance companies often seek to add ancillary services, often ones that are counter-seasonal to the core business. Two examples of such services are snow removal services and holiday lighting. Snow removal services can be highly profitable, but may or may not be considered recurring revenue business, depending on how agreements are structured. If snow removal is provided on an on-demand basis, prices tend to be high, producing good profits when snow events occur. However, in many markets, buyers do not value these revenues as highly because they may not recur every year, depending on weather patterns. In some cases, snow services can be structured on a contractual basis that mitigates this issue. In those cases, snow removal services may be more profitable in seasons in which there are few snow events. Holiday lighting services are also structured in a variety of ways but usually repeat from year-to-year in one way or another. Both snow removal and holiday lighting have the added advantage of enabling the business to retain many of its workers in the off-season, which can have the positive effect of improving employee retention year-to-year.

In general, commercial landscape companies are in greater demand than residential ones. This is due to a variety of factors. There are a number of national and regional companies that are active in acquiring commercial landscape services businesses in select markets. The barriers to entry are also greater for commercial services.

While commercial services are competitive, often very competitive, the competition on the low end of residential services can be extreme, resulting in very low pricing, at least in some markets.

Commercial landscape maintenance businesses tend to attract significant buyer interest, particularly because there are typically relatively few on the market at any point in time.

Residential landscape maintenance businesses typically sell at a lower range than commercial maintenance businesses. Larger residential landscape maintenance businesses tend to sell at higher valuations than smaller ones, largely because they have more effective marketing systems and are able to demonstrate growth and customer retention. They can also operate more efficiently with greater customer density.

In order to maximize the value of the business, the owner can emphasize the value drivers that are relevant to the particular business. For maintenance businesses, some of the drivers that can affect the value of the business include the following:

Landscape Maintenance Businesses

- Quality management and employees.

- A diverse customer base with no single customer or group of customers comprising an inordinate portion of the business.

- A diverse customer base in terms of types or industries of customers.

- A record of retaining customers over an extended period.

- Demonstrated customer satisfaction.

- A scope of services consistent with the competition and with the scope of services desired by likely buyers.

- A billing structure consistent with common practices in the industry (in many markets, equal monthly billing for standard maintenance services year-round).

- Reasonable collection experience.

- An attractive physical facility and equipment.

- Courteous, neat, uniformed employees.

- Good contract pricing producing solid margins consistent with industry benchmarks.
- Good financial records that support the value of the business.

Historically, the demand for commercial landscape maintenance business acquisitions has been cyclical. There have been periods of expansion by consolidators, occasionally resulting in heavy demand and extraordinary prices, followed by periods of limited interest and lower prices. Accordingly, a landscape maintenance business owner anticipating exiting a business by a sale to a third party would be well-advised to prepare the business for sale well in advance of a planned exit timeline and be prepared to make a move when market conditions are favorable.

13

OTHER GREEN INDUSTRY BUSINESSES

In this chapter, we will address unique characteristics in exit planning for some other green industry businesses, including tree care businesses, garden centers and nurseries.

Tree Care

Tree care businesses have some characteristics of landscape, landscape maintenance and lawn care businesses. They often have a recurring revenue component involving fertilization, disease and insect control and pruning. They have a project component, which may be individually bid for tree sales and installation, and they have a nonrecurring service component for specialty diagnosis, service and surgery, and major tree damage issues. The value of a tree care business may vary based on how its business breaks out among these business components.

Some of the drivers that can affect the value of the business include the following:

- An established brand name and reputation for quality services in the marketplace.

Other Green Industry Businesses

- Quality, well-trained and presentable management and employees.

- Appropriate licenses, certification and insurance.

- A diverse customer base with no single customer or group of customers comprising an inordinate portion of the business.

- A diverse customer base in terms of types or industries of customers.

- A record of retaining customers over an extended period.

- Demonstrated customer satisfaction.

- Courteous, well-trained, neat, uniformed employees.

- A well-thought out and consistent pricing strategy.

- Good financial records that support the value of the business.

Garden Centers

In recent years, independent garden centers have been challenging businesses to both operate and sell. The rate of failure within the industry has been high, and the industry continues to be in a state of decline. The decline in garden center performance overall has been caused by poor profit margins, intensifying competition from big box retailers and a decline in discretionary spending as a result of the recession.

Despite the negative operating environment, some garden centers have thrived, and the characteristics of those garden centers suggest value drivers for garden centers. Successful garden centers often have the following characteristics:

- Locations in high growth areas with strong local economies.

- A focus on higher-end consumers who have been less affected by the economic downturn.

- A focus on product lines with higher profit margins, including non-garden products.

- A focus on careful buying to control costs and reduce inventory shrinkage.

- In some cases, a focus on growing its own plant material as a way to reduce costs.

- Adding value-added services with capable, well-trained staff. In some cases, garden centers can add higher margin business like landscaping and plant installation.

Successful garden centers often participate in alliances with other noncompetitive garden centers to make sure their products, services and merchandising practices reflect industry trends and best practices, giving them a competitive edge.

Because many garden centers have exited the industry in recent years, the value attributed to even strongly performing garden centers has, to an extent, been diminished. While the recent economic cycle has taken a significant toll on the garden center industry, it is important to remember that this is a cycle and that there is an opportunity for well-managed, forward-looking garden centers to thrive as the economy rebounds.

Plant and Flower Growers

Plant and flower growers have experienced a negative economic climate for a number of years. This trend is expected to continue in the near term. These businesses have been hit hard by a number of factors, including the following:

- Many of their most significant customers have been retail florists, independent garden centers and landscape businesses, all of which have been hurt by a decrease in discretionary spending during the recession.

- A significant portion of the demand for these products has shifted to big-box retailers like Home Depot, Lowe's and Wal-Mart, which have exerted significant downward pressure on prices along with difficult terms for suppliers.

- The focus on pricing has caused a shift where possible to low-cost foreign producers. The growth of low-cost foreign producers has had the added impact of reducing the demand for export of products from the U.S.

The changing environment for plant and flower growers has created opportunities for industry participants, however. Growers which have some of these characteristics will generate a greater value in the marketplace than others:

- Economies of scale have become very important as growers can leverage their fixed costs and their selling costs over larger operations.

- Transportation costs are a major issue, and growers that can keep this cost low due to regionally located facilities or very large operations which can control their own distribution system are more likely to thrive.

- Growers producing premium and, in some cases, branded products are able to generate higher profit margins.

- The decrease in the number of businesses within the industry has created some opportunities in certain segments, such as large trees, which have a relatively long lead time. The remaining players essentially are protected by a barrier to entry of the time it takes to produce stock.

14

Franchised Businesses

Franchised businesses are very common in various segments of the Green Industry, ranging from some of the biggest players in the industry to newer start-up franchises. Such names as Lawn Doctor, US Lawns, The Grounds Guys, Weed Man, Spring Green, NaturaLawn and many others come to mind, in addition to franchise affiliates of large industry players like TruGreen and Scotts Lawn Service. Franchise business owners are like other business owners – eventually the need to sell or transfer the business will arise. Oftentimes, existing franchises can be very attractive options for business buyers, particularly when dealing with a well-known, successful franchisor. Many buyers will find buying an established business preferable and less risky than buying or launching a start-up with its accompanying start-up losses.

While these franchised businesses are, in many ways, similar to other businesses within the industry, there are some unique issues and concerns which must be addressed when developing an exit strategy.

Franchised Businesses

It is a good idea to communicate with the franchisor early in the relationship about exit planning. Obviously, exit planning is a key concern of franchisees, and many franchisors address issues related to exit planning aggressively up front.

It is also important to understand that the interests of a franchisee and a franchisor with respect to franchisee exit planning may not be totally in sync. The objectives of a franchisee are not very different from any other business owner. The franchisee's objectives will be to be able to exit the business for the best price at the time of his or her choosing and to be able to sell or transfer the business to a buyer of his or her choice.

The franchisor, on the other hand, will be most interested in seeing the franchise operation continue to prosper, generating a steady and increasing stream of royalty payments. The exit of a successful franchisee will create risk to the franchisor and raise concerns.

Right off the bat, one needs to understand the franchisor's attitude toward existing franchise sales. Some companies that have both company-owned and franchised units will be actively engaged in buying back franchises. Some other companies maintain a marketplace through which existing franchisees can identify people interested in acquiring an existing franchise. Some franchisors will support potential sellers through the process, others will ignore them, and still others will try to make the process difficult. Other franchisees may provide the best information about the direction a franchisor will take regarding existing franchise sales.

It will be important to understand and be able to communicate to potential buyers and your advisors exactly what the franchise agreement says about sales of franchised businesses.

Some franchise agreements have a right of first refusal in favor of the franchisor. This provision gives the franchisor the right to match any bid for the business. These common provisions can be very problematical. First, who wants to go to the effort of considering a bid and negotiating on the purchase of a business if their bid can easily be derailed? Second, right of first refusal provisions may give the franchisor an extended period of time to consider whether to exercise the right – sixty days is fairly common. This delay can cause all kinds of problems since few people will want to sit on an offer for sixty days. Franchisors should be encouraged to give a response more quickly.

All franchise agreements will provide that the franchisor has the right to approve the transferee of a franchise. Generally, these agreements are worded to provide that approval cannot be unreasonably withheld. However, this is still another step in the process, and it is important to understand what the franchisor's process related to approving a new franchisee is, including what documents must be submitted and what fees are involved.

The franchisor will need to provide a Franchise Disclosure Document (FDD, formerly known as a Uniform Franchise Offering Circular or UFOC) to the proposed franchisee and comply with applicable federal and state laws in entering into a franchise agreement.

One question that may arise is whether the franchisor will in essence transfer the existing franchise agreement with its existing provisions and term, or enter into a new franchise agreement with the buyer on current forms with current provisions and a full franchise term. If the franchisor can use the most current franchise agreement with the transferee, for example, it is possible that the royalty rates may be different, perhaps higher than for the existing franchisee, which would reduce the cash flow potential of the business and potentially reduce its value.

15

THE ESOP OPTION

One option for an exit strategy for a business owner is to sell the business to an employee stock ownership plan, known by the acronym ESOP.

An ESOP is a special kind of retirement plan for employees that obtains full or partial ownership of a business from a business owner. It serves different purposes for the business owner and its employees. For the business owner, an ESOP is a way to unlock the value of the business on a tax-advantaged basis and transition control of the business to key employees, family members or other insiders. To a business's employees, an ESOP is a retirement plan similar to a 401(K) plan that allows employees a way to share in the success of the company.

ESOPs can be implemented in a variety of ways to accomplish the owner's objectives.

In some cases, ESOPs can be structured as leveraged ESOPs. In a leveraged ESOP, the ESOP borrows money from a financial institution to finance the acquisition of the company's stock from the owner.

The ESOP Option

The business itself guarantees the indebtedness of the ESOP and pledges its assets as collateral for the loan to the ESOP. The business makes regular payments to the ESOP to cover the principal and interest payments on the loan. Because the payments to the ESOP represent pension plan contributions, they will generally be 100% deductible to the company for both the principal and interest portions of the payment.

In other cases, ESOPs are structured without third party financing. The ESOP buys the stock of the Company from the owner with a note. The note is paid with the periodic retirement plan contributions. The stock in the business is released to the ESOP as the note is paid. This approach has the advantage of allowing the business owner to remain involved in day-to-day operations of the business and transfer control of the business to the ESOP over an extended period of time, which often meets the desires and objectives of the business owner.

There are a variety of tax incentives associated with ESOPs:

- The business owner who sells stock to the ESOP pays tax at federal long-term capital gains rates. If the business is a C corporation, the business owner may be able to defer tax, potentially permanently.

- The employees who are participants in the ESOP are not taxed on their allocable shares of the company or its earnings in the ESOP until the shares are distributed at death, disability, retirement or termination.

- The business is generally able to deduct the interest and principal payments on the ESOP loan as retirement plan contributions, subject to applicable limitations.

- C corporations may, in some cases, be able to deduct dividends paid on the ESOP stock.

- S corporations that are owned by ESOPs have a special benefit. S corporations are flow-through entities, and their earnings pass through to their owners for tax purposes. Because the ESOP is not a taxable entity, no tax is payable on its share of the company's earnings.

The ESOP Option

ESOPs are quite popular in the green industry. The Davey Tree Expert Company is the largest employee-owned company in the green industry and one of the largest employee-owned companies in any industry. There are many other ESOPs in the industry, including regional players like The Groundskeeper in Arizona and Jensen Corp. in California.

The case for considering an ESOP can be compelling. Valuations for ESOP purposes tend to be lower than for open-market transactions (partially as a result of the absence of a competitive auction), but the compelling tax benefits, the ability to transition control over a period of time and the ability to transfer ownership to employees and ensure the long-term continuity of the business make the ESOP a compelling option. In particular, ESOPs should be attractive in segments of the industry that may not otherwise command the highest valuations.

Green Exit

16

PRIVATE EQUITY

A private equity firm is an investment manager that makes investments in private companies using funds from investors. Sometimes called a financial sponsor, these firms usually raise funds from investors in pools that are to be invested according to a specific strategy. These funds typically have a limited planned life. Private equity firms receive periodic management fees as well as a share in the profits earned by each fund managed.

Other private equity firms represent the investment arm of wealthy families or individuals. We will call these firms family private equity firms. These firms function similarly to the other firms, except that they do not raise funds from investment pools as the equity is supplied by the owners of the firm.

While all private equity firms will be concerned with an exit strategy from the investments they make, the two types of firms differ in how they view their exit strategy. Firms managing pools of investor money must manage the exit strategy for their investments to enable a return of capital to the fund's investors within the objectives of the fund. Family private equity firms will usually be much more flexible in their attitude toward the timing and nature of exit strategies.

In most cases, private equity investments represent a controlling interest in the business. The original owners and management may also participate in the ownership of the business after a private equity investment.

There has been some interest by private equity firms in the lawn and landscape industry, ranging from very large transactions to fairly small ones. For example, The ServiceMaster Company, which owns TruGreen Lawncare, is currently owned by a group of private equity firms. The Brickman Group, Ltd. has a large investment from private equity. The ValleyCrest Companies have a large investment from a family private equity firm. There are a number of other private equity-owned businesses in both the lawn and landscape industries.

Private equity firms with an interest in the lawn and landscape industry may seek out potential targets directly and privately negotiate transactions. In many cases, however, a business that is interested in seeking a private equity investor will engage a mergers & acquisitions advisory firm to assist it in marketing the business to private equity firms which may be interested. The advisory firm will prepare a confidential information memorandum describing the business and seek proposals from multiple private equity firms. This creates an auction process with the goal of obtaining the best value, deal structure and operational fit for the owners of the business.

Each private equity firm has its own investment parameters, some specializing in very large transactions and others considering much smaller ones. There are only a few private equity firms that will consider a platform acquisition with revenues of less than $20 million with an enterprise value of less than $4 to $5 million and EBITDA (earnings before interest, taxes, depreciation and amortization) less than $1 to $2 million. Many firms will definitely consider smaller acquisitions which represent "tuck-in" or "bolt-on" acquisitions for an existing platform investment.

A private equity investment can be a significant opportunity in exit planning. In some cases, for example, a business owner could seek a private equity investment and partially cash-out his or her ownership interest, allowing the owner to diversify his personal investments. The business owner might retain a key role in the business and an ownership interest with the objective of completing his or her exit at the same time that the private equity firm completes its own exit.

Green Exit

17

PUTTING THE PLAN INTO PLACE

In most cases, there are a variety of exit options available to a business owner, including a sale to a third party and a transfer to an insider. Often, there are a host of further options, including such alternatives as an employee stock ownership plan and a private equity recapitalization. Based on the owner's objectives and a realistic assessment of the value of the business, the business owner can identify the option or options that are most likely to best satisfy his or her objectives.

It is now time to pull the plan together. As has already been illustrated in this book, there are many factors and options to consider in developing the plan.

The completed plan should include the following parts:

- A restatement of the business owner's objectives in developing the exit plan and a statement of his or her plans post-exit.

- An assessment of the value of the business as it currently stands and what steps are expected to be necessary to unlock that value.

PUTTING THE PLAN INTO PLACE

- A specific plan to improve the value and salability of the business based on an examination of the business, its value drivers and market conditions, currently and in the foreseeable future.

- A specific plan to preserve the value of the business against risks and uncertainties that exist or may develop between the time the plan is developed and the time the plan is to be executed.

- A specific plan, customized for the situation, to unlock the value of the business by completing a sale or transfer of the business in the future, including a description of the plan, steps that must be taken to execute the plan and a planned timeframe or milestones which must be reached to execute the plan.

- And perhaps, most importantly, a process for updating the plan for changing circumstances.

As the plan is completed, you will have assembled many of the resources and advisors you will need to execute the plan when the time comes. Because you will have familiarized your team of advisors with your objectives and the facts about your business, they will be in a much better position to advise you about steps to take in the future. They will also be ready when you make the decision to proceed with a sale or transfer *on your terms and on your timeframe*.

A key part of the plan will be to include a process for updating and revising the plan for changing facts and circumstances. Among the changes that will often require modification of the plan are the following:

- Family changes, including marriage, births and death.

- Health issues.

- Positive or negative changes in the business.

- Positive or negative changes in the overall industry.

- Positive or negative changes in the overall economy.

- Changes in the business owner's attitude toward specific potential buyers or transferees.

- Competitive issues.

- Changes in the business owner's personal plans post-exit.

- Changes in the business owner's financial assets other than the business.

- Changes in federal, state and local taxes.

Many of these changes are inevitable. Without updating the plan for changes, the plan's value to the business owner greatly diminishes in value. One approach that many business owners find useful is to schedule an annual review of the exit plan, either as part of an overall planning process or as a part of a year-end financial review.

Green Exit

18

CHOOSING ADVISORS

The advisors you choose will have a big impact on the development of your exit plan and, ultimately, the success of the sale or transfer of your business.

You may need an exit planning specialist, a financial planner, an attorney, a tax advisor, an accountant and a business broker or other intermediary. Some professionals may play more than one role: an exit planning specialist may also be an attorney, accountant or business broker and a tax advisor may also be an attorney or an accountant.

Exit Planning Specialist

Exit planning specialists have special training and experience to assist clients with developing an exit plan. Some exit planning specialists function only in that role, and others are also attorneys, accountants or business brokers. An exit planning specialist is trained to assist his or her clients in understanding both their objectives and the facts about their personal financial situation and the business's value and salability. That information then provides the basis for developing a reasonable and achievable exit plan for the individual's circumstances.

Financial Planner

There are important roles for a financial planning advisor to play in connection with the develop of an exit plan. This professional should be able to assess the value of your current financial assets and recommend alternatives as to how a potential transaction could be structured and the proceeds invested in order to achieve your financial goals post-exit.

Attorneys, Accountants and Tax Advisors

While you probably already have an attorney and an accountant, it is a good idea to consider whether you have the right advisors in place to advise you in connection with an exit strategy and the possible sale of your business.

The attorney you choose to advise you with respect to exit planning may or may not be different from the one you use for routine legal matters. It is important for him or her to have specific experience with similar kinds of transactions and to be comfortable working with the advisors who will be working with the buyer. An attorney is ethically bound to work in your best interest, but he or she may not agree with you or your other advisors on what that best interest is. Some attorneys may be sticklers for issues that you may or may not consider important. The most important things are that your attorney has your best interests in mind, is experienced in the type of transaction you are contemplating and is, by disposition, a "deal-maker" as opposed to a "deal-breaker." It is also important that your attorney has the time available to serve you well.

The tax advisor you choose (who may be your attorney, your accountant or another advisor) will mostly work with you in planning to structure a potential transaction in the best possible way. He or she will need to have your confidence, ideally already be at least generally familiar with your tax situation, have appropriate experience and have the time available to serve you while the plan is being developed and, ultimately, when a transaction is being negotiated.

Your accountant will need to be able to assist in providing documents needed by your other advisors and be committed to timely assistance. This may result in a change in the timing of the services provided in the past, especially if tax returns have been extended as much as possible. When the time comes, the buyers will need to see financial information and tax returns that are current.

Working with Business Brokers

Most business owners considering the sale of their business will find it desirable to engage the services of a business broker, consultant or other intermediary. The compelling reasons to use a broker include:

- The business broker focuses on the sale of the business, allowing the business owner to focus on the continued operations of the business being sold, thus maintaining its value through the process.

- The business sale process can be complex and confusing, partly because most business owners only go through it one or two times in a lifetime.

- The business broker is in a better position than the business owner to maintain confidentiality through the process, which is usually a goal of the business owner.

- The business broker can give the business owner objective advice throughout the process.

- The business broker can assist the owner with telling the story of the business in the most appealing way to various potential buyers.

- The business broker acts as an intermediary, focusing on the big picture of moving a transaction forward to successful completion. In this role, he or she assists in smoothing waters, tying up loose ends, working out differences and resolving other issues that inevitably develop.

The business brokerage industry is comparatively new and undeveloped. In most states, there is no restriction on who can call themself a business brokers. A few states license business brokers directly, and another handful may require a real estate license. (A real estate license may be required for transactions involving real estate.)

Some business brokers represent sellers; some business brokers represent buyers; and some others seem to represent both buyers and sellers at the same time.

In selecting a business broker or merger & acquisition advisor to work with, the following considerations may be helpful:

- Does the business broker have a good reputation? Can he or she supply references?

- Is the business broker a member of industry organizations, such as the International Business Brokers Association, the Association for Corporate Growth or similar organizations?

- Is the business broker well-known within your industry, with a large network of contacts?

- Does the business broker represent the interests of the seller, the buyer or both?

Some business brokers or consultants state that their fees are always paid by the business buyer. This may sound attractive, but you can be very sure that the buyer factors in the cost of the business broker into his or her analysis of the business being acquired. In this case, the seller may not even know the amount the broker is being paid or its impact on the offer he receives from the buyer. To be sure, an experienced broker may well still be able to get the best price in a deal. However, you have to ask yourself if a broker being paid by the business buyer will have the seller's best interests at heart.

Business brokers involved in the exit planning process will charge a consulting fee to their clients. This consulting fee may either be an hourly rate or a flat fee covering a specific scope of services.

Most business brokers are paid with a commission on the sale price of the business. The higher the sale price, the higher their commission. Some business brokers, especially those being paid by business buyers, are paid a commission based on the revenues of the business acquired as opposed to the sale price. This structure is often used when a broker attempts to represent the interests of both the buyer and seller.

In addition, many business brokers charge a retainer to begin the engagement and may have fees for other services rendered in connection with an engagement, including reimbursement of out-of-pocket expenses. Because the process of selling a business can be lengthy, many business brokers charge an up-front retainer to cover their costs in initiating the engagement and may charge periodic fees during the engagement. These fees may or may not be deducted from the commission (sometimes called a "success fee") charged when the business is sold.

The important things to remember in dealing with business brokers include:

- Make sure the business broker or intermediary you work with is reputable.

- Make sure you have a clear understanding of whose interests the business broker represents and what you can expect.

- Make sure you have a clear understanding of the business broker's fees and when they are to be paid.

- Make sure the business broker is committed to clear and open communication about the entire process and the progress being made.

19

AN EXIT PLANNING CHECKLIST

This checklist is intended to guide you through the exit planning process and to stimulate your thoughts as to topics you may not have considered.

1. After exiting your business, do you expect (1) to retire, (2) to start or buy another business or (3) to become an employee of another business?

2. Have you analyzed your financial readiness to exit the business?

3. If you plan to retire, have you analyzed your financial requirements in retirement and how they will be met?

4. If you are planning to start or buy another business, have you analyzed the financial requirements associated with that endeavor?

5. If you are planning to become an employee of another business, have you analyzed your living requirements and how they will be met through a combination of compensation and other sources, including investments and proceeds from the sale of your business?

6. In almost all cases, when a business is sold, the seller will be required to enter into a noncompetition

agreement with the buyers of the business. If you are planning to start or buy another business or to become an employee of another business, have you considered whether a noncompetition agreement will affect the new business?

7. Do you consider yourself mentally ready to exit the business? If not, what steps will you take to prepare yourself mentally for exiting the business?

8. Have you identified the team of professionals to assist you with exit planning? E.g., Exit Planning Specialist, Attorney, Accountant, Tax Advisor, Wealth Planner, Business Intermediary or Business Broker? *(Some advisors may fill more than one role, and not all roles may be necessary in every situation.)*

9. If everything were perfect, when would you like to exit your business?

10. Do you have a realistic understanding of the value of your business?

11. Do you have an understanding of the value drivers of your business?

12. Have you considered what steps you can take to improve the value and salability of your business and developed a plan to address them?

13. Have you considered and taken steps to preserve the value of your business between now and the time you plan to exit the business? Have you considered what can go wrong and how to minimize its effect?

14. Have you identified the exit planning options that are most likely to meet your personal objectives?

15. Have you completed an exit plan to guide you from now until you exit your business?

16. Have you established a process for regularly reviewing and updating your exit plan for changes in your objectives, your personal situation, the progress of the business and market conditions?

17. Have you considered what is most important to you? Rank the following objectives in order from most important to least important to you.

____Selling your business at the highest possible price

____Selling your business to the best possible buyer

____Transferring the business to a family member or family members

____Transferring the business to a key employee or employees

An Exit Planning Checklist

____Making sure your employees have an opportunity for continued employment

____Making sure your customers continue to be served in the way that you think they should be

____Having a stable income after exiting your business

____Minimizing the tax consequences of selling your business

About the Author

Ron Edmonds is principal of The Principium Group, Inc. His practice focuses on mergers & acquisitions and related services, including advising clients on matters related to exit strategy planning and capital formation. He has extensive background in all phases of the merger and acquisition process. In addition to fourteen years in public accounting, he served as chief financial officer for a company executing a consolidation strategy. He has participated as an advisor or intermediary in well over 300 acquisitions during the past ten years.

He is a frequent author and speaker on topics related to green industry mergers and acquisitions. He is the editor of **Green Industry Merger & Acquisition News**, a monthly newsletter tracking the industry, and

SellMyGreenBusiness.com, an educational website. He has been a speaker for continuing education programs for over twenty-five years. He has written articles for a variety of industry publications.

Mr. Edmonds' other books include *Charting a Course – Vivant Landscape Considers Acquisitions*, *How to Sell Your Green Business—A Guide for Green Industry Business Owners* and *A Toolkit for Selling Your Green Business*.

Mr. Edmonds is an adjunct faculty member of the School of Business at Christian Brothers University. He currently teaches MBA-level courses in Entrepreneurship.

He is a certified public accountant (Oklahoma, inactive) and a member of the Association for Corporate Growth, the Association of Professional Mergers & Acquisitions Advisors, the Professional Landcare Network and the International Business Brokers Association. He holds BS and MS degrees in accounting from the Spears School of Business at Oklahoma State University.

About the Author

To schedule a consultation, Mr. Edmonds can be reached at 888-229-5740 or by sending email to redmonds@principiumgroup.com.

About The Principium Group

The Principium Group, Inc. is a leading advisory firm serving the green industry in the areas of mergers & acquisitions, exit planning and capital formation.

Principium professionals have assisted buyers and sellers in hundreds of transactions in a variety of industries, including consumer services, financial services, medical practices and others. They are located in the Memphis, Tennessee, area, but serve clients on a national basis.

Principium focuses on serving clients in the Green Industry, including landscape services, lawn maintenance, irrigation and related businesses. In these areas, we serve clients on a national basis. The Firm's professionals participate regularly in industry events and conferences.

Principium serves both buyers and sellers in mergers and acquisitions. For buyers, Principium provides assistance and counsel in strategic planning, identifying potential acquisition targets, conducting due diligence investigations and planning for successful integration of acquisitions. For sellers, Principium provides assistance and counsel in evaluating strategic alternatives, identifying and negotiating with potential acquirers and assisting with transactions from due diligence through the closing process. Principium also assists companies and their investors and financing sources with restructuring to achieve a profitable level of operations.

In addition to advising business buyers and sellers, The Principium Group provides educational material through its informational website SellMyGreenBusiness.com and its monthly electronic newsletter **Green Industry Merger & Acquisition News**. It also offers regularly scheduled workshops and seminars open to industry business leaders and offers custom-designed training for individual businesses and associations.

About the Author

Principium professionals participate actively in key trade associations related to mergers & acquisitions, including the Association for Corporate Growth, the International Business Brokers Association and the Association of Professional Mergers & Acquisitions Advisors. Where appropriate, Principium cooperates with other organizations to bring the widest possible exposure to our clients. Their broad industry experience and background is your advantage as you plan for the future of your business, whether or not you are presently contemplating the sale of your business or adding to your existing business by acquiring another one.

Principium Group professionals understand that the decision to sell your business is a profound decision, and pledge to work with you in a professional and confidential manner while helping you navigate this often confusing process. Whether you have immediate plans to buy or sell a business or may sometime in the future, they welcome the opportunity to talk with you about your business.

Contact them by email at info@principiumgroup.com, by telephone at 888-229-5740, or on the web at www.PrincipiumGroup.com.

www.ingramcontent.com/pod-product-compliance
Lightning Source LLC
Chambersburg PA
CBHW061509180526
45171CB00001B/104